USBORNE
ROUND
THE
WORLD
IN SPANISH

First published in 1980
Usborne Publishing Ltd
20 Garrick Street
London WC2E 9BJ, England

© Usborne Publishing Ltd 1980

Printed and bound in Great Britain

About this book

This book is for everyone learning Spanish. By looking at the pictures, it will be easy to read and learn the words underneath them.

Masculine and Feminine Words

When you look at the words in Spanish, you will see that most of them have **la** or **el,** which means 'the', in front of them. When learning Spanish, it is a good idea to learn the **la** or **el** with each word. This is because all Spanish words, like bicycle and train, as well as man and woman, are masculine or feminine. **La** usually means the word is feminine and **el** that it is masculine. If the word is plural — that is, there is more than one thing, such as bicycles or trains, then it has **las** or **los** in front of it. **Las** is the feminine and **los** is the masculine.

Looking at the words

Some Spanish words have an **n** in them with a squiggle over it, like this ñ. It is called a tilde. In Spanish this ñ is a separate letter of the alphabet and is said differently from the ordinary **n**. Some letters also have accents on them. This does not change the sound of the letter but changes the way the word is spoken.

Saying the words

At the back of the book there is a guide to pronouncing every word in the pictures. This is to help you say them. But there are some sounds in Spanish which are quite different from any sounds in English. To say them as a Spanish person would, you have to hear them spoken. Listen very carefully and then try to say them like that yourself. But if you say them as they are written in the pronunciation guide, a Spanish person will understand you — even if your Spanish accent is not quite perfect.

Can you find the dog?

On every picture across two pages there is a spotty dog to look for. Can you find it?

USBORNE
ROUND
THE
WORLD
IN SPANISH

With Easy Pronunciation Guide

Carol Watson and Dolores Bereijo
Illustrated by David Mostyn

Pronunciation guide by Geoffrey K. Pullum

En la ciudad

la iglesia

el garaje

la casa

el parque

la parada
de autobús

los
semáforos

el paso
de peatones

el anuncio

la señal
de tráfico

el hotel

la fábrica

la tienda

la chimenea

el camarero

el parque
de bomberos

el coche
de bomberos

4

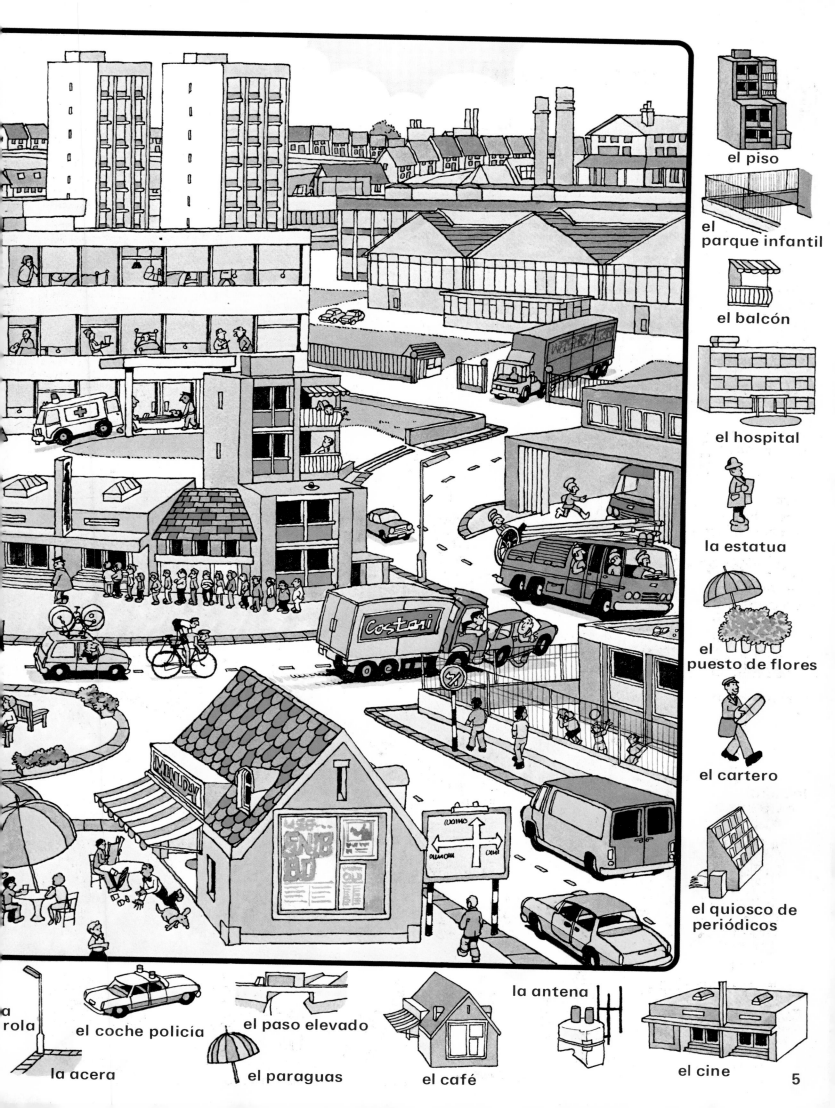

el piso

el parque infantil

el balcón

el hospital

la estatua

el puesto de flores

el cartero

el quiosco de periódicos

la antena

la rola

el coche policía

el paso elevado

la acera

el paraguas

el café

el cine

5

En movimiento

el tren

la rikisha

el biplano

la furgoneta

la bicicleta

el camión para caballerías

el carro de caballos

el globo de aire caliente

el coche deportivo

el autobús

el transportador

el camión cisterna

el hang-glider

el monoraíl

el tanque

el remolque

6

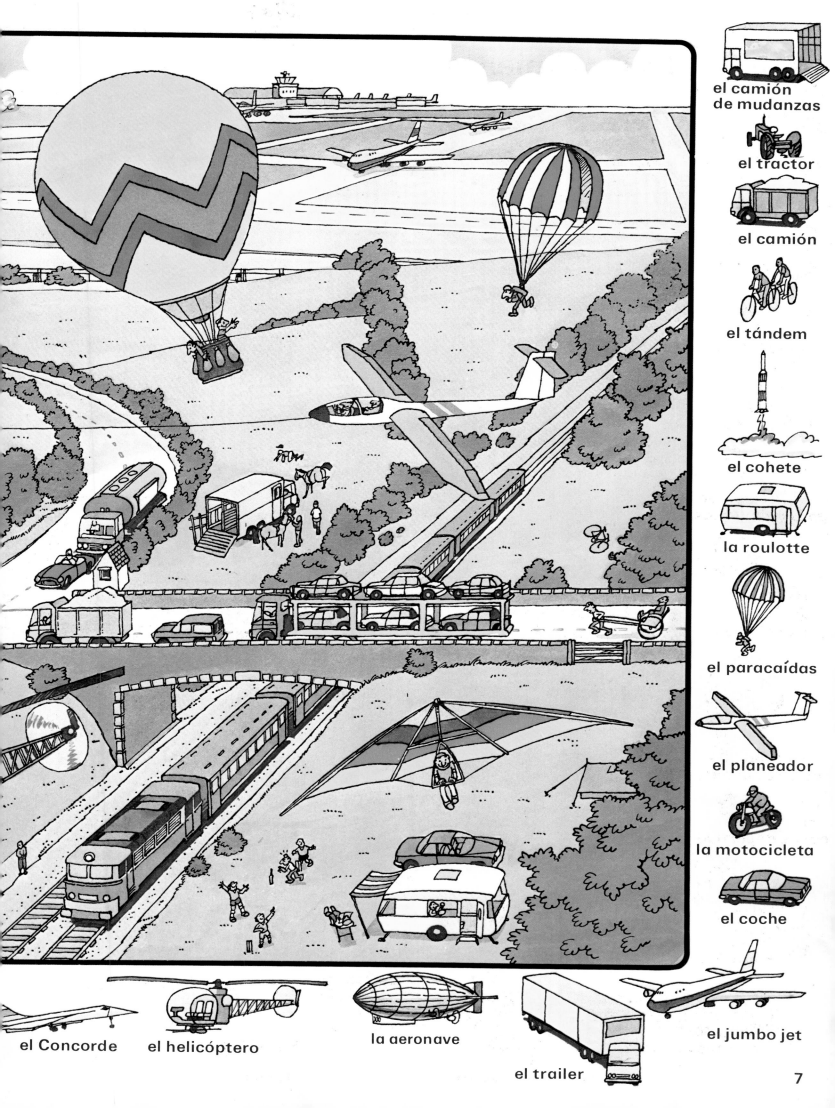

el camión
de mudanzas

el tractor

el camión

el tándem

el cohete

la roulotte

el paracaídas

el planeador

la motocicleta

el coche

el jumbo jet

el Concorde   el helicóptero   la aeronave

el trailer

7

En el agua

la red

el cesto

el río

la presa pesquera

el canal

las espadañas

la canoa

el puente

la caña

el sedal

el pescador

8 la tumbona

la barcaza

el pato

el patito

el acueducto

la balsa

la puerta
de esclusa

la motora

el motor
fuera-bordo

la lancha
neumática

el malecón

el cobertizo
para botes

los juncos

la vivienda
flotante

el canalete

el corcho

el yate de motor

el cisne

el bote de remos

el remo

9

En el puerto

el remolcador

el aerodeslizador

la grúa

el bolardo

el almacén

la boya

el saco

la caja

la portilla

el submarino

10

el estibador

la gabarra

la chimenea

el transbordador

el envase

la bandera

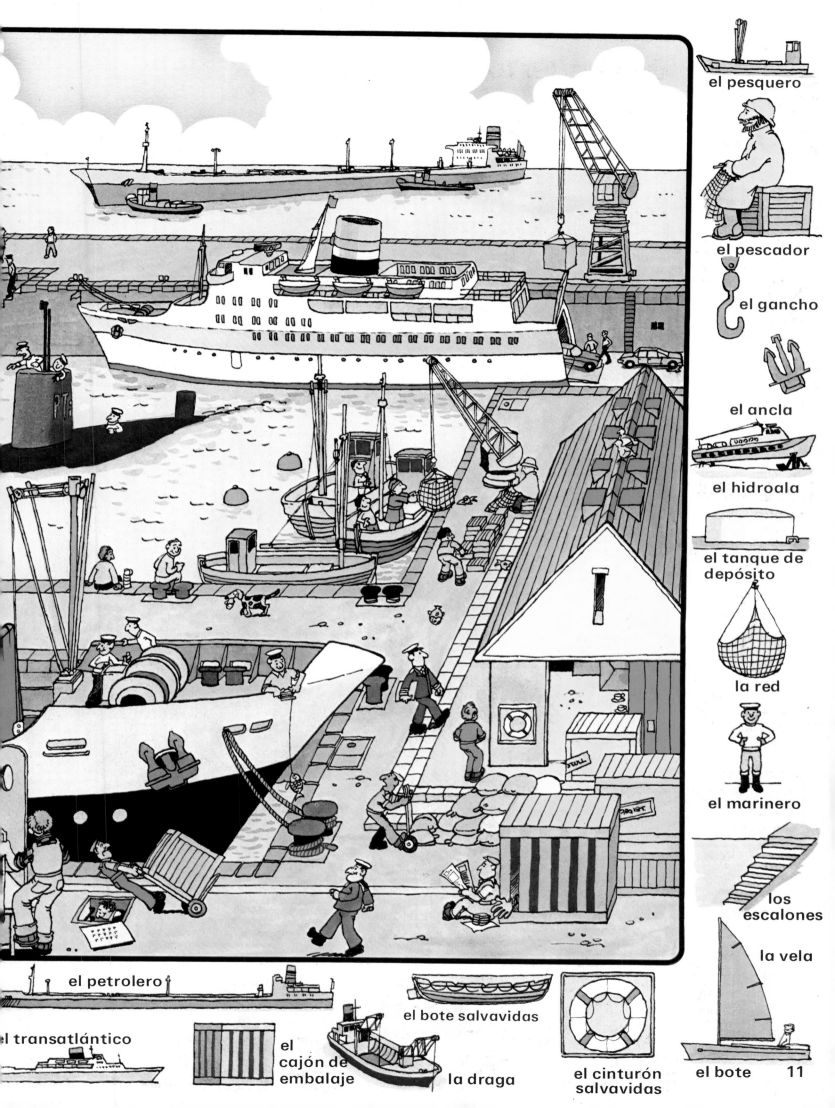

el pesquero

el pescador

el gancho

el ancla

el hidroala

el tanque de depósito

la red

el marinero

los escalones

la vela

el petrolero

el bote salvavidas

el transatlántico

el cajón de embalaje

la draga

el cinturón salvavidas

el bote

11

En la sierra

la roca

el alpinista

la cuerda

la oveja

la cabra

el águila

el pico

el piolet

el glaciar

el puma

el esquí

las piedras

el abeto

la cueva

el mapa

el caminante

12

el telesquí

el canto rodado

la mochila

la cascada

el oso   el osezno

los cuernos

el alce de América

la cabãna de troncos

el bosque

el leñador

os prismáticos

el tronco

la sierra

las botas de escalar

el hacha

13

En el desierto

el burro

la silla
de montar

la rata canguro

el nómada

el camello

el zorro del
desierto

el pozo
petrolífero

el avestruz

el antílope

el halcón

la arena

la duna

el espino

el pozo

la tortuga
del desierto

la gacela

el jeep

la palmera

la manta

la calavera

el esqueleto

la culebra

la liebre

el buitre

el lirio
del desierto

la
ormiga

la tienda

el oasis

el lagarto

el escorpión

15

Bajo el agua

el tiburón

la aleta

el pez

la escafandra

las botellas
de oxígeno

la playa

los guijarros

la esponja

la roca

el naufragio

el cofre del tesoro

la cuerda

la cueva

la
estrella de mar

16

el cangrejo

la langosta

la concha

las algas

la ostra

la anémona de mar

el caballito de mar

la burbuja

el pulpo

el tentáculo

la medusa

la aleta

el equipo de buzo

el buzo

En la jungla

el gorila

el bambú

la enredadera

el tucán

la araña

la flecha

el cazador

la rana de San Antonio

la mariposa

18 la canoa

el científico

la seta

el jaguar

el chimpancé

el camaleón

la culebra

el murciélago

el tapir

el mono

el cocodrilo

el lémur

el perezoso

el loro

las huellas

la orquídea

el colibrí

el tronco de árbol

la hoja

el puente de cuerdas

el oso hormiguero

19

Tierras frías

el iceberg

el hielo

el perro esquimal

la capucha

el arpón

los anteojos

el carámbano

el muñeco de nieve

la bola de nieve

el iglú

20 el esquiavión

el rompehielos

la golondrina de mar

la foca

el kayac

el reno

la morsa

el oso polar

la nieve

el tractor de nieve

el trineo

la ballena

el zorro blanco

el snow-cat

la lechuza blanca

las raquetas de nieve

las manoplas

el trineo a motor

el esquimal

21

El carnaval

el escudo

el tambor

la hoguera

el aro

el acróbata

la bruja

el malabarista

la peluca

la bufanda

la borla

el estandarte

el penacho

la máscara

el casco

la linterna

la capa

los fuegos artificiales

la bailarina

los zancos

el palo de escoba

el payaso

el pendiente

el dosel

pluma

los globos

la llama

las espuelas

la vela

la lanza

la bandera

el carruaje

La música

la trompa

el tambor

los palillos

las castañuelas

la pandereta

el oboe

el triángulo

la guitarra eléctrica

el atril

el director

el órgano

la cítara

la concertina

el acordeón

el xilófono

el bajón

la trompeta

la armónica

el violoncelo

la tuba

la balalaica

el violín

el arco

el saxofón

los platillos

el arpa

el dulce

las maracas

la gaita

la campanilla

la guitarra

el trombón

el clarinete

el banjo

la flauta

el contrabajo

el piano

25

Comidas y bebidas

el pincho moruno

la tortita

el perrito caliente

el pavo

el melocotón

las ostras

las patatas fritas

la manzana

el helado

las salchichas de Frankfurt

los espaguetis

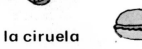

la ciruela

la hamburguesa

el pan

la leche

el tomate

el café

las fresas

la cerveza

el bocadillo

el queso

el pescado

la empanada

el té

el vino

el pastel

la gelatina   la pera   las cerezas   los caracoles   el maíz

la limonada

el arroz

la ensalada

27

la falda
hawaiana

las botas

el kimono

los pantalones
vaqueros

la pajarita

el caftán

la gorra

la sotana

la boina

28

Vestidos

la capa

el sombrero
hongo

el bolero

las zapatillas

el chal

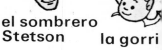

el sombrero
Stetson

la gorri

el chandal

el sombrero
de copa

el poncho

la
falda escocesa

el sombrero

el sari

el fez

el velo de
musulmana

el turbante

las sandalias

el sombrero
de culí

las chaparreras

hábito

el frac

el esmoquin

los
zuecos

el
traje espacial

29

Los cultivos

el tabaco

el arroz

los dátiles

el trigo

las coles

los cocos

los tulipanes

el algodón

las uvas

el cacao

el té

las piñas

los girasoles

el café

la madera

la caña de azucar

los plátanos

31

Peligros

el iceberg

las arenas movedizas

el maremoto

el volcán

el terremoto

el huracán

la tromba marina

el incendio forestal

la avalancha

el relámpago

la ventisca

el tornado

la tempestad de arena

la inundación

Casas y viviendas

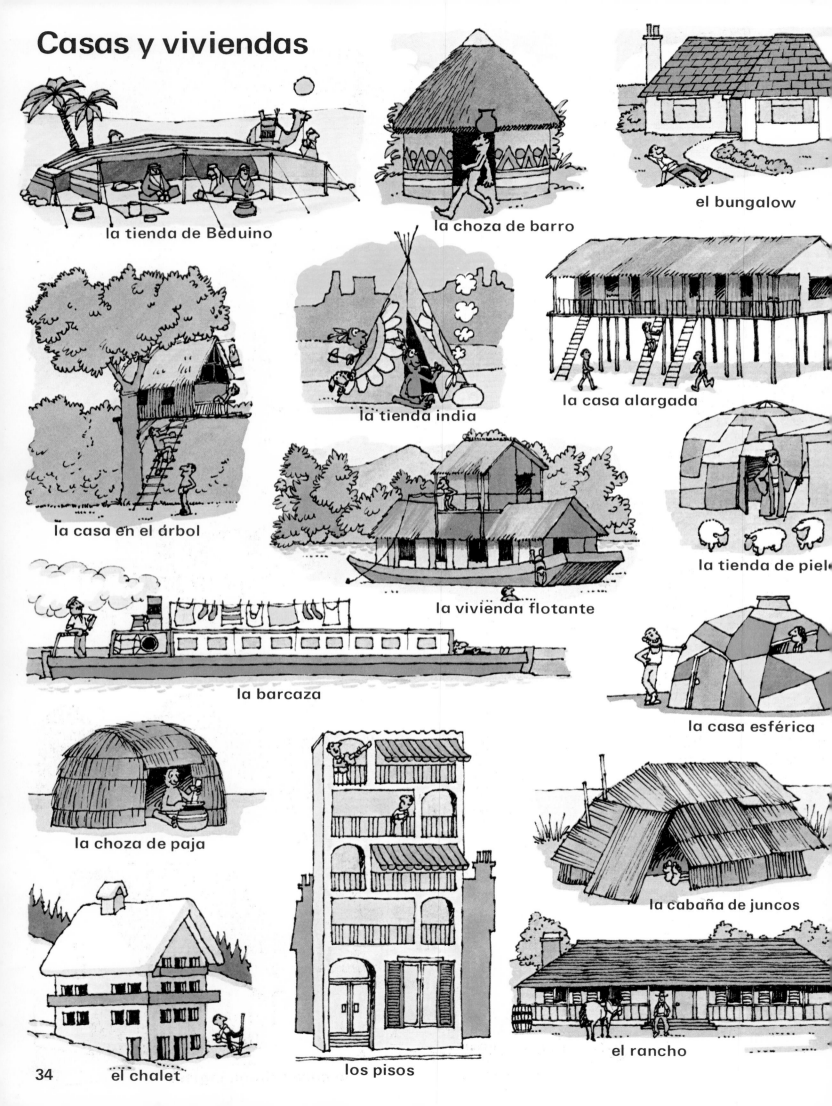

la tienda de Beduino

la choza de barro

el bungalow

la casa en el árbol

la tienda india

la casa alargada

la tienda de piel

la vivienda flotante

la barcaza

la casa esférica

la choza de paja

la cabaña de juncos

el chalet

los pisos

el rancho

la casa de papel

la granja

el faro

el carro de gitanos

la cueva

la casita de campo

el palafito

el castillo

el fuerte

la cabaña de troncos

el sampán

la casa urbana inglesa

35

Animales

el wombat

el coala

el bisonte

el orangután

el tití

el león

el casto

el yak

el galápago

el hipopótamo

el mapache

la cebra

el delfín

el elefante

el tejón

la ardilla listada

el gibón

el panda gigante

la llama

el tigre

la mofeta

el ñu

el lémur

el puerco-espín

el armadillo

la hiena

el mandril

el canguro

la jirafa

el lobo

el leopardo

el rinoceronte

37

Edificios y lugares famosos

**1 el castillo de Luis de Baviera
— Alemania**

**2 el puente 'Puerta de Oro'
— América**

**3 la torre inclinada de Pis
— Italia**

**4 la Mezquita Azul
— Irán**

**5 el palacio de la ópera de Sydney
— Australia**

**6 las cataratas del Niágara
— América y Canadá**

**7 el Everest
— Nepal**

**8 la Torre Eiffel
— Francia**

38

**9 Stonehenge (monumento neolítico)
— Inglaterra**

**10 la catedral de San Basilio
— Rusia**

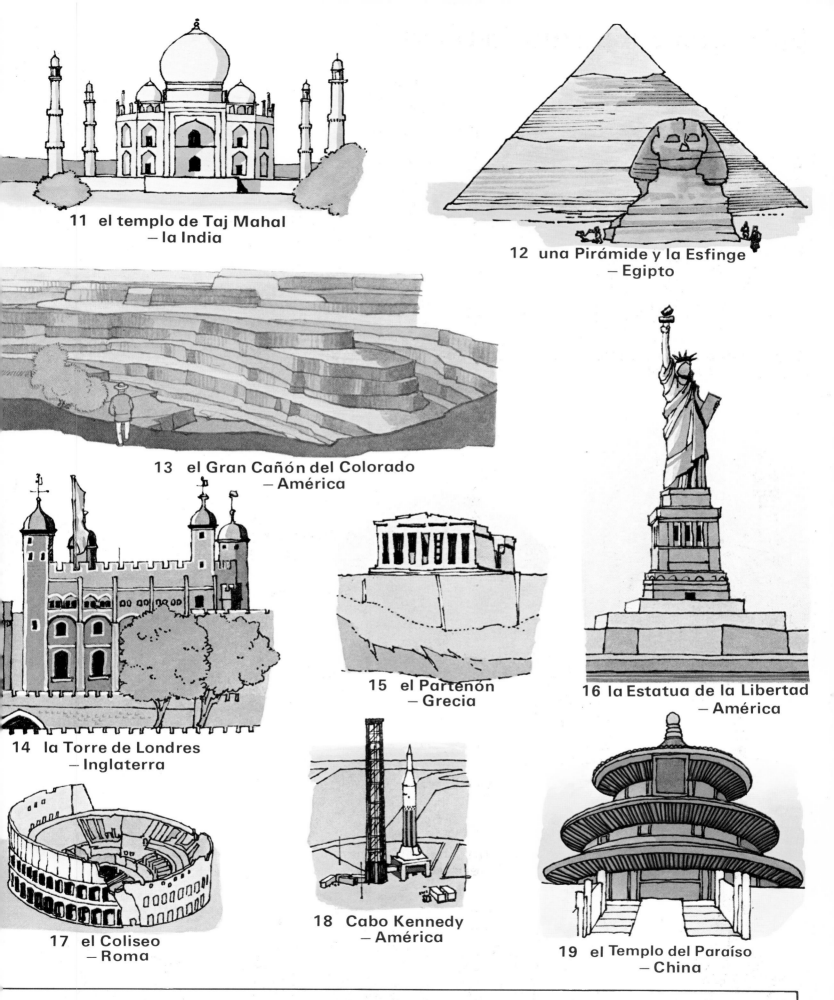

11 el templo de Taj Mahal
— la India

12 una Pirámide y la Esfinge
— Egipto

13 el Gran Cañón del Colorado
— América

14 la Torre de Londres
— Inglaterra

15 el Partenón
— Grecia

16 la Estatua de la Libertad
— América

17 el Coliseo
— Roma

18 Cabo Kennedy
— América

19 el Templo del Paraíso
— China

Look at the map on the next two pages. Match up the numbers to find out where the buildings and places are in the world.

El mapamundi

ALASKA

el esquimal

GROENLANDIA

el iglú

OCÉANO ÁRTICO

el barco de pesca

CANADÁ

9 14

8

ESTADOS UNIDOS DE AMÉRICA

el cohete

6

16

2

13

18

el aerodeslizador

1

3

17

EUROPA

15

el Concorde

OCÉANO ATLÁNTICO

AFRICA

SUDAMÉRICA

el transatlántico

OCÉANO PACÍFICO

Can you name the animals?

You can find them in this book.

el bote

40

The numbers on the map show where the famous buildings and places are to be found. See pages 38 and 39.

el globo de aire caliente

RUSIA

OCÉANO PACÍFICO

el maremoto

19

CHINA

7

el submarino

4

11

el pozo petrolífero

LA INDIA

el petrolero

el jumbo jet

AUSTRALIA

el helicóptero

NUEVA ZELANDA

el rompehielos

LA ANTÁRTIDA

el snowcat

41

Index

This is the alphabetical list of all the words in the pictures in this book. The Spanish alphabet is a little different to English. All words beginning with **ch** come at the end of the **c**'s. Words beginning with **ll** are at the end of the **l**'s and words beginning with **ñ** at the end of the **n**'s. The Spanish word comes first, then there is the pronunciation in *italics,* followed by the English translation.
The pronunciation guide shows how the words are pronounced in Spain. (In Latin America it is a little bit different.) The sounds of Spanish are not exactly the same as the sounds of English, so the only way to pronounce Spanish in exactly the right way is to listen to Spanish people speaking and imitate them. However, the following list will be some help in getting the sounds roughly correct.

ah — stands for a sound like the *a* in *calm*
eh — stands for a sound like the *e* in *get*
oh — stands for a sound like the *o* in *so*
ee — stands for a sound like the *ee* in *seen*
oo — stands for a sound like the *oo* in *soon*
au — roughly rhymes with the *ow* of *cow*
ai — roughly rhymes with the *i* of *fine*
th — always sounds like the *th* of *thin* (never like *the*)
s — always sounds like the *s* of *so* (never like *rose*)
y — always sounds like the *y* of *yes* (never like *my*)
g — always sounds like the *g* of *go* (never like *George*)
kh — stands for a sound like the *ch* of *loch* the way Scots people pronounce it.

There are two different r-sounds:
r — stands for a short *r*-sound made with one flap of the tongue.
rr — is like the *r*-sound you use to say *brr!* when it is very cold

It is important to stress the right part of the word in Spanish, so the stressed part of each word is shown in capital letters.

Spanish	Pronunciation	English
el bosque	el BOHS-keh	forest
la bota	lah BOH-tah	boot
las botas (f)	lahs BOH-tahs	boots
las botas de escalar (f)	lahs BOH-tahs deh ehs-kah-LAHR	climbing boots
el bote	el BOH-teh	dinghy
el bote de remos	el BOH-teh deh REH-mohs	rowing boat
el bote salvavidas	el BOH-teh sahl-vah-VEE-dahs	lifeboat
las botellas de oxígeno (f)	lahs boh-TEH-lyahs deh ohk-SEE-kheh-noh	aqualung
la boya	lah BOH-yah	buoy
la bruja	lah BROO-khah	witch
la bufanda	lah boo-FAHN-dah	scarf
el buitre	el BWEE-treh	vulture
el bungalow	el boong-GAH-loh	bungalow
la burbuja	lah boor-BOO-khah	bubble
el burro	el BOO-rroh	donkey
el buzo	el BOO-thoh	diver
el caballito de mar	el kah-bah-LYEE-toh deh MAHR	seahorse
la cabaña de juncos	lah kah-BAH-nyah deh KHOONG-kohs	reed house
la cabaña de troncos	lah kah-BAH-nyah deh TROHNG-kohs	log cabin
Cabo Kennedy	KAH-boh KEH-neh-dee	Cape Kennedy
la cabra	lah KAH-brah	goat
el cacao	el kah-KAH-oh	cocoa
el café	el kah-FEH	café, coffee
el caftán	el kahf-TAHN	kaftan
la caja	lah KAH-khah	box
el cajón de embalaje	el kah-KHOHN deh em-bah-LAH-kheh	crate
la calavera	lah kah-lah-BEH-rah	skull
el camaleón	el kah-mah-leh-OHN	chameleon
el camarero	el kah-mah-REH-roh	waiter
el camello	el kah-MEH-lyoh	camel
el caminante	el kah-mee-NAHN-teh	walker
el camión	el kah-mee-OHN	lorry
el camión cisterna	el kah-mee-OHN thee-STEHR-nah	petrol tanker
el camión de mudanzas	el kah-mee-OHN deh moo-DAHN-thahs	removal van
el camión para caballerías	el kah-mee-OHN pah-rah kah-bah-lyeh-REE-ahs	horsebox
la campanilla	lah kahm-pah-NEE-lyah	hand bell
Canadá	kah-na-DAH	Canada
el canal	el kah-NAHL	canal
el canalete	el kah-nah-LEH-teh	paddle
el cangrejo	el kahng-GREH-khoh	crab
el canguro	el kahng-GOO-roh	kangaroo
la canoa	lah kah-NOH-ah	canoe
el canto rodado	el KAHN-toh roh-DAH-doh	boulder
la caña	lah KAH-nyah	rod
la caña de azúcar	lah KAH-nyah deh ah-thoo-KAHR	sugar cane
la capa	lah KAH-pah	cloak
la capucha	lah kah-POO-chah	hood
el caracol	el kah-rah-KOHL	snail
los caracoles (m)	lohs kah-rah-KOH-lehs	snails

Spanish	Pronunciation	English
el carámbano	el kah-RAHM-bah-noh	icicle
el carnaval	el kahr-nah-VAHL	carnival
el carro de caballos	el KAH-rroh deh kah-BAH-lyohs	horse and cart
el carro de gitanos	el KAH-rroh deh khi-TAH-nohs	gypsy caravan
el carruaje	el kah-roo-AH-kheh	carriage
el cartero	el kahr-TEH-roh	postman
la casa	lah KAH-sah	house
la casa alargada	lah KAH-sah ah-lahr-GAH-dah	long house
la casa de papel	lah KAH-sah deh pah-PEL	paper house
la casa en el árbol	lah KAH-sah en el AHR-bohl	tree house
la casa esférica	lah KAH-sah ehs-FEH-ree-kah	dome house
la casa urbana inglesa	lah KAH-sah oor-BAH-nah ing-GLEH-sah	terraced house
casas y viviendas	KAH-sahs ee bee-BYEHN-dahs	houses and homes
la cascada	lah kahs-KAH-dah	waterfall
el casco	el KAHS-koh	helmet
la casita de campo	lah kah-SEE-tah deh KAHM-poh	cottage
las castañuelas (f)	lahs kah-stah-NYWEH-lahs	castanets
el castillo	el kah-STEE-lyoh	castle
el castillo de Luis de Baviera	el kah-STEE-lyoh deh loo-EES deh bah-BYEH-rah	Ludwig's Castle
el castor	el kah-STOHR	beaver
las cataratas del Niágara (f)	lahs kah-tah-RAH-tahs del nee-AH-gah-rah	Niagara Falls
la catedral de San Basilio	lah kah-teh-DRAHL deh sahn bah-SEE-lyoh	St Basil's Cathedral
el cazador	el kah-thah-DOHR	hunter
la cebra	lah THEH-brah	zebra
la cereza	lah theh-REH-thah	cherry
las cerezas (f)	lahs theh-REH-thahs	cherries
la cerveza	lah thehr-BEH-thah	beer
el cesto	el THEHS-toh	hamper
el científico	el thyen-TEE-fee-koh	scientist
el cine	el THEE-neh	cinema
el cinturón salvavidas	el theen-too-ROHN sahl-bah-BEE-dahs	lifebelt
la ciruela	lah theer-WEH-lah	plum
el cisne	el THEES-neh	swan
la cítara	lah THEE-tah-rah	sitar
la ciudad	lah thee-oo-DAHD	city
el clarinete	el klah-ree-NEH-teh	clarinet
el coala	el koh-AH-lah	koala bear
el cobertizo para botes	el koh-behr-TEE-thoh pah-rah BOH-tehs	boathouse
el coco	el KOH-koh	coconut
el cocodrilo	el koh-koh-DREE-loh	crocodile
el coche	el KOH-cheh	car
el coche de bomberos	el KOH-cheh deh bohm-BEH-rohs	fire engine
el coche deportivo	el KOH-cheh deh-pohr-TEE-boh	sports car
el coche policía	el KOH-cheh poh-lee-THEE-ah	police car
el cofre del tesoro	el KOH-freh del teh-SOH-roh	treasure chest

Spanish	Pronunciation	English
el cohete	*el koh-EH-teh*	rocket
la col	*lah KOHL*	cabbage
las coles (f)	*lahs KOH-lehs*	cabbages
el colibrí	*el koh-lee-BREE*	humming bird
el Coliseo	*el koh-lee-SEH-oh*	The Colosseum
la comida	*lah koh-MEE-dah*	food
comidas y bebidas	*koh-MEE-dahs EE beh-BEE-dahs*	food and drink
la concertina	*lah kohn-thehr-TEE-nah*	concertina
el Concorde	*el kohn-KOHR-deh*	Concorde
la concha	*lah KOHN-chah*	shell
el contrabajo	*el kohn-trah-BAH-khoh*	double bass
el corcho	*el KOHR-choh*	float
la cuerda	*lah KWEHR-dah*	rope
los cuernos (m)	*lohs KWEHR-nohs*	antlers
la cueva	*lah KWEH-bah*	cave house, cave
la culebra	*lah koo-LEH-brah*	snake
los cultivos (m)	*lohs kool-TEE-bohs*	crops
el chal	*el CHAHL*	shawl
el chalet	*el chah-LEHT*	chalet
el chandal	*el CHAHN-dahl*	tracksuit
las chaparreras (f)	*lahs chah-pah-RREH-rahs*	chaps
la chimenea	*lah chee-meh-NEH-ah*	chimney, funnel
el chimpancé	*el cheem-pahn-THEH*	chimpanzee
China	*CHEE-nah*	China
la choza de barro	*lah CHOH-thah deh BAH-rroh*	mud hut
la choza de paja	*lah CHOH-thah deh PAH-kha*	grass hut
los dátiles (m)	*lohs DAH-tee-lehs*	dates
el delfín	*el del-FEEN*	dolphin
el desierto	*el deh-SYEHR-toh*	desert
el director	*el dee-rek-TOHR*	conductor
el dosel	*el doh-SEHL*	canopy
la draga	*lah DRAH-gah*	dredger
el dulce	*el DOOL-theh*	recorder
la duna	*lah DOO-nah*	dune
el edificio	*el eh-dee-FEE-thee-oh*	building
edificios y lugares famosos	*eh-dee-FEE-thee-ohs ee loo-GAH-rehs fah-MOH-sohs*	famous buildings and places
Egipto	*eh-KHEEP-toh*	Egypt
el elefante	*el eh-leh-FAHN-teh*	elephant
la empanada	*lah em-pah-NAH-dah*	pie
la enredadera	*lah en-reh-dah-DEH-rah*	creeper
la ensalada	*lah en-sah-LAH-dah*	salad
el envase	*el en-BAH-seh*	container
el equipo de buzo	*el eh-KEE-poh deh BOO-thoh*	wetsuit
la escafandra	*lah ehs-kah-FAHN-drah*	mask (of a diver)
los escalones (m)	*lohs ehs-kah-LOH-nehs*	steps
el escorpión	*el eh-skohr-PYOHN*	scorpion
el escudo	*el eh-SKOO-doh*	shield
el esmoquin	*el eh-SMOH-keen*	tuxedo
las espandañas (f)	*lahs eh-spah-DAH-nyahs*	bulrushes
los espaguetis (m)	*lohs eh-spah-GEH-tees*	spaghetti
el espino	*el eh-SPEE-noh*	thornbush
la esponja	*lah eh-SPOHNG-khah*	sponge
las espuelas (f)	*lahs eh-SPWEH-lahs*	spurs
el esqueleto	*el eh-skeh-LEH-toh*	skeleton
el esquí	*el eh-SKEE*	ski
el esquiavión	*el eh-skee-ah-BYOHN*	ski plane
el esquimal	*el eh-skee-MAHL*	Eskimo
Estados Unidos de América (E.E.U.U.)	*eh-STAH-dohs oo-NEE-dohs deh ah-MEH-ree-kah (eh eh oo oo)*	United States of America
el estandarte	*el eh-stahn-DAHR-teh*	banner
la estatua	*lah eh-STAH-twah*	statue
la Estatua de la Libertad	*lah eh-STAH-twah deh lah lee-behr-TAHD*	The Statue of Liberty
el estibador	*el eh-stee-bah-DOHR*	docker
la estrella de mar	*lah eh-STREH-lyah deh MAHR*	starfish
Europa	*eh-oo-ROH-pah*	Europe
el Everest	*el eh-beh-REHST*	Mount Everest
la fábrica	*lah FAH-bree-kah*	factory
la falda escocesa	*lah FAHL-dah eh-skoh-THEH-sah*	kilt
la falda hawaiana	*lah FAHL-dah ah-wah-YAH-nah*	grass skirt
famoso	*fah-MOH-soh*	famous
el faro	*el FAH-roh*	lighthouse
la farola	*lah fah-ROH-lah*	lamp post
el fez	*el FEHTH*	fez
la flauta	*lah FLAU-tah*	flute
la flecha	*lah FLEH-chah*	arrow
la foca	*lah FOH-kah*	seal
el frac	*el FRAHK*	tailcoat
Francia	*FRAHN-thyah*	France
la fresa	*lah FREH-sah*	strawberry
las fresas (f)	*lahs FREH-sahs*	strawberries
frío	*FREE-oh*	cold
los fuegos artificiales (m)	*lohs FWEH-gohs ahr-tee-fee-thee-AHL-ehs*	fireworks
el fuerte	*el FWEHR-teh*	fort
la furgoneta	*lah foor-goh-NEH-tah*	van
la gabarra	*lah gah-BAH-rrah*	barge
la gacela	*lah gah-THEH-lah*	gazelle
la gaita	*lah GAI-tah*	bagpipes
el galápago	*el gah-LAH-pah-goh*	giant tortoise
el gancho	*el GAHN-choh*	hook
el garaje	*el gah-RAH-kheh*	garage
la gelatina	*lah kheh-lah-TEE-nah*	jelly
el gibón	*el khee-BOHN*	gibbon
los girasoles (m)	*lohs khee-rah-SOH-lehs*	sunflowers
el glaciar	*el glah-THYAHR*	glacier
el globo	*el GLOH-boh*	balloon
el globo (de aire caliente)	*el GLOH-boh (deh AI-reh kahl-YEN-teh)*	hot air balloon
la golondrina de mar	*lah goh-lohn-DREE-nah deh MAHR*	tern
el gorila	*el goh-REE-lah*	gorilla
la gorra	*lah GOH-rrah*	cap
la gorrita	*lah goh-RREE-tah*	bonnet
el Gran Cañón del Colorado	*el GRAHN kah-NYOHN del koh-loh-RAH-doh*	The Grand Canyon
la granja	*lah GRAHNG-khah*	farmhouse
Grecia	*GREH-thyah*	Greece

Groenlandia	groh-ehn-LAHN-dyah	Greenland
la grúa	lah GROO-ah	crane
el guijarro	el gee-KHAH-rroh	pebble
los guijarros (m)	lohs gee-KHAH-rrohs	pebbles
la guitarra	lah gee-TAH-rrah	guitar
la guitarra electrica	lah gee-TAH-rrah eh-LEHK-tree-kah	electric guitar
el hábito	el ah-BEE-toh	habit
el hacha	el AH-chah	axe
el halcón	el ahl-KOHN	hawk
la hamburguesa	lah ahm-boor-GEH-sah	hamburger
el hang glider	el ahng-glee-DEHR	hang glider
el helado	el eh-LAH-doh	ice cream
el helicóptero	el eh-lee-KOHP-teh-roh	helicopter
el hidroala	el ee-droh-AH-lah	hydrofoil
el hielo	el YEH-loh	ice
la hiena	lah YEH-nah	hyena
el hipopótamo	el ee-poh-POH-tah-moh	hippopotamus
la hoguera	lah oh-GEH-rah	bonfire
la hoja	lah OH-khah	leaf
la hormiga	lah ohr-MEE-gah	ant
el hospital	el oh-spee-TAHL	hospital
el hotel	el oh-TEL	hotel
las huellas (f)	lahs WEH-lyahs	tracks
el huracán	el oo-rah-KAHN	hurricane
el iceberg	el ee-theh-BEHRG	iceberg
la iglesia	lah ee-GLEH-syah	church
el iglú	el ee-GLOO	igloo
el incendio forestal	el een-THEHN-dyoh foh-reh-STAHL	forest fire
India	EEN-dyah	India
Inglaterra	eeng-glah-TEH-rrah	England
la inundación	lah een-oon-dah-THYOHN	flood
Irán	ee-RAHN	Iran
Italia	ee-TAH-lyah	Italy
el jaguar	el kha-GWAHR	jaguar
el jeep	el KHEEP	jeep
la jirafa	lah khee-RAH-fah	giraffe
el jumbo jet	el KHOOM-boh KHEHT	jumbo jet
los juncos (m)	lohs KHOONG-kohs	reeds
la jungla	lah KHOONG-glah	jungle
el kayac	el kah-YAHK	kayak
el kimono	el kee-MOH-noh	kimono
el lagarto	el lah-GAHR-toh	lizard
la lancha neumática	lah LAHN-chah neh-oo-MAH-tee-kah	rubber dinghy
la langosta	lah lahng-GOH-stah	lobster
la lanza	lah LAHN-thah	spear
la leche	lah LEH-cheh	milk
la lechuza blanca	lah leh-CHOO-thah BLAHNG-kah	snowy owl
el lémur	el LEH-moor	lemur
el leñador	el leh-nya-DOHR	lumberjack
el león	el leh-OHN	lion
el leopardo	el leh-oh-PAHR-doh	leopard
la liebre	lah lee-EH-breh	hare
la limonada	lah lee-moh-NAH-dah	lemonade
la linterna	lah leen-TEHR-nah	lantern
el lirio del desierto	el LEE-ryoh del deh-SYEHR-toh	desert lily

el lobo	el LOH-boh	wolf
el loro	el LOH-roh	parrot
el lugar	el loo-GHAHR	place
la llama	lah LYAH-mah	flame, llama
la madera	lah mah-DEH-rah	timber
el maíz	el mah-EETH	corn
el malabarista	el mah-lah-bah-REE-stah	juggler
el malecón	el mah-leh-KOHN	jetty
el mandril	el mahn-DREEL	baboon
las manoplas (f)	lahs man-NOH-plahs	mittens
la manta	lah MAHN-tah	blanket
la manzana	lah mahn-THAH-nah	apple
el mapa	el MAH-pah	map
el mapache	el mah-PAH-cheh	racoon
el mapamundi	el mah-pah-MOON-dee	map of the world
las maracas (f)	lahs mah-RAH-kahs	maracas
el maremoto	el mah-reh-MOH-toh	tidal wave
el marinero	el mah-ree-NEH-roh	sailor
la mariposa	lah mah-ree-POH-sah	butterfly
la máscara	lah MAH-skah-rah	mask
la medusa	lah meh-DUH-sah	jellyfish
el melocotón	el meh-loh-koh-TOHN	peach
La Mezquita Azul	lah mehth-KEE-tah ah-THOOL	The Blue Mosque
la mochila	lah moh-CHEE-lah	haversack
la mofeta	lah moh-FEH-tah	skunk
el mono	el MOH-noh	monkey
el monorail	el moh-noh-RAIL	monorail
la morsa	lah MOHR-sah	walrus
la motocicleta	lah moh-toh-thee-KLEH-tah	motorcycle
el motor fuera-bordo	el moh-TOHR FWEH-rah BOHR-doh	outboard motor
la motora	lah moh-TOH-rah	motorboat
el movimiento	el moh-bee-MYEHN-toh	movement
el muñeco de nieve	el moo-NYEH-koh deh nee-EH-beh	snowman
el murciélago	el moor-thee-EH-lah-goh	bat
la música	lah MOO-see-kah	music
el naufragio	el nau-FRAH-kyoh	wreck
Nepal	neh-PAHL	Nepal
la nieve	lah nee-EH-beh	snow
el nómada	el NOH-mah-dah	nomad
Nueva Zelanda	NWEH-bah theh-LAHN-dah	New Zealand
el ñu	el NYOO	gnu
el oasis	el oh-AH-sees	oasis
oboe	el oh-BOH-eh	oboe
Océano Artico	oh-THEH-ah-noh ahr-TEE-koh	Arctic Ocean
Océano Atlántico	oh-THEH-ah-noh aht-LAHN-tee-koh	Atlantic Ocean
Océano Pacifico	oh-THEH-ah-noh pah-THEE-fee-koh	Pacific Ocean
el orangután	el oh-rahng-oo-TAHN	orang-utan
el órgano	el OHR-gah-noh	organ
la orquídea	lah ohr-KEE-deh-ah	orchid
el osezno	el oh-SEHTH-noh	bear cub
el oso	el OH-soh	bear

Spanish	Pronunciation	English
el oso hormiguero	el OH-soh ohr-mee-GEH-roh	anteater
el oso polar	el OH-soh poh-LAHR	polar bear
la ostra	lah OH-strah	oyster
las ostras (f)	lahs OH-strahs	oysters
la oveja	lah oh-BEH-kha	sheep
la pajarita	lah pah-khah-REE-tah	bow tie
El Palacio de la ópera de Sydney	el pah-LAH-thyoh deh lah OH-peh-rah deh SEED-nee	The Sydney Opera House
el palafito	el pah-lah-FEE-toh	stilthouse
los palillos (m)	lohs pah-LEE-lyohs	drumsticks
la palmera	lah pahl-MEH-rah	palm tree
el palo de escoba	el PAH-loh deh eh-SKOH-bah	broomstick
el pan	el PAHN	bread
el panda gigante	el PAHN-dah khee-GAHN-teh	giant panda
la pandereta	lah pahn-deh-REH-tah	tambourine
los pantalones vaqueros (m)	lohs pahn-tah-LOH-nehs bah-KEH-rohs	jeans
el paracaídas	el pah-rah-kah-EE-dahs	parachute
la parada de autobús	lah pah-RAH-dah deh au-toh-BOOS	bus stop
el paraguas	el pah-RAH-gwahs	umbrella
el parque	el PAHR-keh	park
el parque de bomberos	el PAHR-keh deh bohm-BEH-rohs	fire station
el parque infantil	el PAHR-keh een-fahn-TEEL	playground
el Partenón	el pahr-teh-NOHN	The Parthenon
el paso de peatones	el PAH-soh deh peh-ah-TOH-nehs	crossing
el paso elevado	el PAH-soh eh-leh-BAH-doh	flyover
el pastel	el pah-STEHL	gateau
las patatas fritas (f)	lahs pah-TAH-tahs FREE-tahs	chips
el patito	el pah-TEE-toh	duckling
el pato	el PAH-toh	duck
el pavo	el PAH-boh	turkey
el payaso	el pah-YAH-soh	clown
el peligro	el peh-LEE-groh	danger
la peluca	lah peh-LOO-kah	wig
el penacho	el peh-NAH-choh	plume
el pendiente	el pehn-DYEHN-teh	earring
la pera	lah PEH-rah	pear
el perezoso	el peh-reh-THOH-soh	sloth
el perrito caliente	el peh-RREE-toh kah-lee-EHN-teh	hotdog
el perro esquimal	el PEH-rroh eh-skee-MAHL	husky dog
el pescado	el peh-SKAH-doh	fish
el pescador	el peh-skah-DOHR	fisherman
el pesquero	el peh-SKEH-roh	fishing boat
el petrolero	el peh-troh-LEH-roh	oil tanker
el pez	el PEHTH	fish
el piano	el PYAH-noh	piano
el pico	el PEE-koh	peak
la piedra	lah PYEH-drah	stone
las piedras (f)	lahs PYEH-drahs	stones
el pincho moruno	el PEEN-choh moh-ROO-noh	shish kebab
la piña	lah PEE-nyah	pineapple
el piolet	el pyoh-LEHT	ice axe
Pirámide y la Esfinge	pee-RAH-mee-deh ee lah ehs-FEENG-kheh	Pirámide and the Sphinx
el piso	el PEE-soh	flat,
los pisos (m)	lohs PEE-sohs	flats
el planeador	el plah-neh-ah-DOHR	glider
los plátanos (m)	lohs PLAH-tah-nohs	bananas
los platillos (m)	lohs plah-TEE-lyohs	cymbals
la playa	lah PLAH-yah	sand (beach)
la pluma	lah PLOO-mah	feather
el poncho	el POHN-choh	poncho
la portilla	lah pohr-TEE-lyah	porthole
el pozo	el POH-thoh	well
el pozo petrolífero	el POH-thoh peh-troh-LEE-feh-roh	oil well
la presa pesquera	lah PREH-sah peh-SKEH-rah	weir
los prismáticos (m)	lohs prees-MAH-tee-kohs	binoculars
el puente	el PWEHN-teh	bridge
el puente de cuerdas	el PWEHN-teh deh KWEHR-dahs	rope bridge
el puente "Puerta de Oro"	el PWEHN-teh PWEHR-tah deh OH-roh	The Golden Gate Bridge
el puerco espín	el PWEHR-koh ehs-PEEN	porcupine
la puerta de esclusa	lah PWEHR-tah deh eh-SKLOO-sah	lockgates
el puerto	el PWEHR-toh	harbour, port
el puesto de flores	el PWEH-stoh deh FLOH-rehs	flower stall
el pulpo	el POOL-poh	octopus
el puma	el POO-mah	puma
el queso	el KEH-soh	cheese
el quiosco de periódicos	el kee-OH-skoh deh pehr-YOH-dee-kohs	newspaper stand
la rana de San Antonio	lah RAH-nah deh SAHN ahn-TOHN-yoh	tree frog
el rancho	el RAHN-choh	ranch house
las raquetas de nieve (f)	lahs rah-KEH-tahs deh nee-EH-beh	snowshoes
la rata canguro	lah RAH-tah kahng-GOO-roh	kangaroo rat
la red	lah REHD	net
el relámpago	el reh-LAHM-pah-goh	lightning
el remo	el REH-moh	oar
el remolcador	el reh-mohl-kah-DOHR	tug
el remolque	el reh-MOHL-keh	trailer
el reno	el REH-noh	reindeer
el rikisha	el ree-KEE-sah	rickshaw
el rinoceronte	el ree-noh-theh-ROHN-teh	rhinoceros
el río	el REE-oh	river
la roca	lah ROH-kah	rock
el rompehielos	el rohm-peh-YEH-lohs	icebreaker
la roulotte	lah roh-oo-LOH-teh	caravan
Rusia	ROO-syah	Russia
el saco	el SAH-koh	sack
las salchichas de Frankfurt (f)	lahs sahl-CHEE-chahs deh frahngk-FOORT	frankfurters
el sampán	el sahm-PAHN	sampan
las sandalias (f)	lahs sahn-DAHL-yahs	sandals
el sari	el SAH-ree	sari

Spanish	Pronunciation	English
el saxofón	el sahk-soh-FOHN	saxophone
el sedal	el seh-DAHL	fishing line
los semáforos (m)	lohs seh-MAH-foh-rohs	traffic lights
la señal de trafico	lah seh-NYAHL deh TRAH-fee-koh	road sign
la seta	lah SEH-tah	mushroom
la sierra	lah SYEH-rrah	saw, mountains
la silla de montar	lah SEE-lyah deh mohn-TAHR	saddle
el snow-cat	el snoh-KAHT	snowcat
el sombrero	el sohm-BREH-roh	sombrero
el sombrero de copa	el sohm-BREH-roh deh KOH-pah	top hat
el sombrero de culi	el sohm-BREH-roh deh koo-LEE	coolie hat
el sombrero hongo	el sohm-BREH-roh OHNG-goh	bowler hat
el sombrero stetson	el sohm-BREH-roh STEHT-sohn	stetson
la sotana	lah soh-TAH-nah	cassock
Stonehenge	stohn-eh-EHNG-kheh	Stonehenge
el submarino	el soob-mah-REE-noh	submarine
Sudamérica	soo-dah-MEH-ree-kah	South America
el tabaco	el tah-BAH-koh	tobacco
el tambor	el tahm-BOHR	drum
el tándem	el TAHN-dehm	tandem
el tanque	el TAHNG-keh	tank
el tanque de depósito	el TAHNG-keh deh deh-POH-see-toh	storage tank
el tapir	el tah-PEER	tapir
el té	el TEH	tea
el tejón	el teh-KHOHN	badger
el telesquí	el teh-leh-SKEE	ski lift
la tempestad de arena	lah tehm-peh-STAHD deh ah-REH-nah	sandstorm
el templo de Taj Mahal	el TEHMP-loh deh TAHKH mah-AHL	The Taj Mahal
el Templo del Paraíso	el TEHMP-loh del pah-rah-EE-soh	The Temple of Heaven
el tentáculo	el tehn-TAH-koo-loh	tentacle
el terremoto	el teh-rreh-MOH-toh	earthquake
el tiburón	el tee-boo-ROHN	shark
la tienda	lah TYEHN-dah	shop, tent
la tienda de Beduino	lah TYEHN-dah deh beh-DWEE-noh	tent (Bedouin)
la tienda de pieles	lah TYEHN-dah deh PYEH-lehs	yurt
la tienda india	lah TYEHN-dah EEN-dyah	wigwam
la tierra	lah TYEH-rrah	land
tierras frias	TYEH-rrahs FREE-ahs	cold lands
el tigre	el TEE-greh	tiger
el tití	el tee-TEE	marmoset
el tomate	el toh-MAH-teh	tomato
el tornado	el tohr-NAH-doh	tornado
La Torre de Londres	lah TOH-rreh deh LOHN-drehs	The Tower of London
La Torre Eiffel	lah TOH-rreh ee-FEHL	The Eiffel Tower
La torre inclinada de Pisa	lah TOH-rreh een-klee-NAH-dah deh PEE-sah	The Leaning Tower of Pisa
la tortita	lah tohr-TEE-tah	pancake
la tortuga del desierto	lah tohr-TOO-gah del deh-SYEHR-toh	desert turtle
el tractor	el trahk-TOHR	tractor
el tractor de nieve	el trahk-TOHR deh nee-EH-beh	snow tractor
el trailer	el trai-LEHR	juggernaut
el traje espacial	el TRA-kheh eh-spah-THYAHL	space suit
el transatlántico	el trahns-aht-LAHN-tee-koh	liner
el transbordador	el trahns-bohr-dah-DOHR	ferry boat
el transportador	el trahns-pohr-tah-DOHR	transporter
el tren	el TREHN	train
el triángulo	el tree-AHNG-goo-loh	triangle
el trigo	el TREE-goh	corn
el trineo	el tree-NEH-oh	sledge
el trineo a motor	el tree-NEH-oh ah moh-TOHR	snowmobile
la tromba marina	lah TROHM-bah mah-REE-nah	waterspout
la trombón	lah trohm-BOHN	trombone
la trompa	lah TROHM-pah	French horn
la trompeta	lah trohm-PEH-tah	trumpet
el tronco	el TROHNG-koh	log
el tronco de árbol	el TROHNG-koh deh AHR-bohl	tree trunk
la tuba	lah TOO-bah	tuba
el tucán	el too-KAHN	toucan
el tulipán	el too-lee-PAHN	tulip
los tulipanes (m)	lohs too-lee-PAH-nehs	tulips
la tumbona	lah toom-BOH-nah	deckchair
el turbante	el toor-BAHN-teh	turban
las uvas (f)	lahs OO-bahs	grapes
la vela	lah BEH-lah	candle, sail
el velo de musulmana	el BEH-loh deh moo-sool-MAH-nah	yashmak
la ventisca	lah behn-TEE-skah	blizzard
los vestidos (m)	lohs beh-STEE-dohs	clothes
el vino	el BEE-noh	wine
el violín	el byoh-LEEN	violin
el violoncelo	el byoh-lohn-THEH-loh	cello
la vivienda	lah bee-BYEHN-dah	house, home
la vivienda flotante	lah bee-BYEHN-dah floh-TAHN-teh	houseboat
el volcán	el bohl-KAHN	volcano
el wombat	el wohm-BAHT	wombat
el xilófono	el see-LOH-foh-noh	xylophone
el yak	el YAHK	yak
el yate de motor	el YAH-teh deh moh-TOHR	cabin cruiser
los zancos (m)	lohs THAHNG-kohs	stilts
las zapatillas (f)	lahs thah-pah-TEE-lyahs	slippers
el zorro blanco	el THOH-rroh BLAHNG-koh	white fox
el zorro del desierto	el THOH-rroh del deh-SYEHR-toh	desert fox
los zuecos (m)	lohs THWEH-kohs	clogs